IN THIS ISSUE:

ISSUE 05 MAY 2017

PUBLISHER
Tourism Tattler (Pty) Ltd.
PO Box 891, Umhlanga Rocks, 4320
KwaZulu-Natal, South Africa.
Website: www.tourismtattler.com

EXECUTIVE EDITOR Des Langkilde
Cell: +27 (0)82 374 7260
Fax: +27 (0)86 651 8080
E-mail: editor@tourismtattler.com
Skype: tourismtattler

MAGAZINE ADVERTISING
ADVERTISING DIRECTOR Bev Langkilde
Cell: +27 (0)71 224 9971
Fax: +27 (0)86 656 3860
E-mail: bev@tourismtattler.com
Skype: bevtourismtattler

SUBSCRIPTIONS
http://eepurl.com/bocldD

BACK ISSUES (Click on the covers below).

▼ APR 2017 ▼ MAR 2017 ▼ FEB 2017

▼ JAN 2017 ▼ DEC 2016 ▼ NOV 2016

▼ OCT 2016 ▼ SEP 2016 ▼ AUG 2016

▼ JUL 2016 ▼ JUN 2016 ▼ MAY 2016

CONTENTS

EDITORS DESK
03 Supporting the IYSTD17 initiative

AFRICA: SUSTAINABLE TOURISM
06 Fair Trade Tourism Joins IYSTD17 initiative
07 Eco & Sustainable Tourism Icons
08 Tips on Greening your Tourism Business

SOUTH AFRICA: ECO-FRIENDLY HOTELS & LODGES
10 Jaci's Lodges
11 Hotel Verde
12 Karongwe Portfolio

ATTRACTIONS
14 Developing Tourism Routes

AVIATION
16 The Vertical Potential Of Airport Transfers

BUSINESS & FINANCE
17 SATSA Market Intelligence Report
18 Are South A'fricas Room Rates Sustainable?

DESTINATIONS
20 Reunion Island: Tropical Incentive with a French Touch

EVENTS
23 Medical Tourism Certification - Added Value Or Waste Of Money?

MARKETING
24 Protecting the Female Traveller
25 The Hidden Power of Ritual
26 All You Need to Know About Email Marketing

NICHE TOURISM
30 A Guide to Cultural Tourism

EDITORIAL CONTRIBUTORS

Angeliki Katsapi   Martin Janse van Vuuren
Anita Mendiratta   Marlien Lourens
Carey Finn   Peter Tarlow
Des Langkilde   Yvonne Nhuta

MAGAZINE SPONSORS

02 The Hotel Show Africa   11 Hotel Verde
05 Pan-African Health Tourism Congress 12 Karongwe Portfolio
09 Hotel Verde, Cape Town   10 Lalibela Private Game Reserve
10 Jaci's Lodges   20 Réunion Island Tourism Board

SUPPORTED CHARITIES

29 Diabetes South Africa   32 National Sea Rescue Institute

Disclaimer: The Tourism Tattler is published by Tourism Tattler (Pty) Ltd and is the official trade journal of various trade 'associations' (see page 02). The Tourism Tattler digital e-zine, is distributed free of charge to bona fide tourism stakeholders. Letters to the Editor are assumed intended for publication in whole or part and may therefore be used for such purpose. The information provided and opinions expressed in this publication are provided in good faith and do not necessarily represent the opinions of Tourism Tattler (Pty) Ltd, its 'Associations', its staff and its production suppliers. Advice provided herein should not be soley relied upon as each set of circumstances may differ. Professional advice should be sought in each instance. Neither Tourism Tattler (Pty) Ltd, its 'Associations', its staff and its production suppliers can be held legally liable in any way for damages of any kind whatsoever arising directly or indirectly from any facts or information provided or omitted in these pages or from any statements made or withheld or from supplied photographs or graphic images reproduced by the publication.

BUSINESS EVENT MEDIA PARTNER

VISION CONFERENCE
WHERE EXPERTS DISCUSS & DEBATE MARKET CHALLENGES, OPPORTUNITIES AND TRENDS

LIVE FEATURES:
CAFÉ CULTURE
LOVE DESIGN
MIXOLOGY CHALLENGE

100s OF GLOBAL BRANDS

THE Hotel Show AFRICA

100% HOSPITALITY
for hotel, restaurant, café and foodservice professionals

25 - 27 JUNE 2017
GALLAGHER CONVENTION CENTRE
JOHANNESBURG, SOUTH AFRICA

REGISTER ONLINE NOW FOR FREE ENTRY!
www.thehotelshowafrica.com

Co-located with:

Strategic Partners:

Powered by:

Organised by:

EDITORIAL

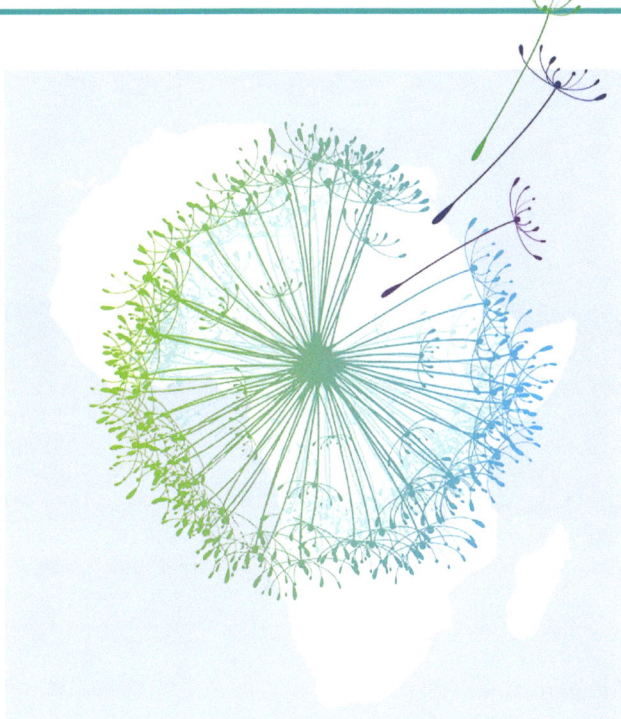

> **Every year, 1.2 billion people travel abroad. These, and the billions more who travel domestically, create a sector which contributes 10% of global GDP to the world's economies and 1 in 11 jobs. Tourism has become a passport to prosperity, a driver of peace, and a transformative force for improving millions of lives.**
>
> **Taleb Rifai - UNWTO Secretary General.**

SUPPORTING THE 2017 INTERNATIONAL YEAR OF SUSTAINABLE TOURISM FOR DEVELOPMENT

As an international influence for travel in the content of Africa, Tourism Tattler has joined global media in promoting the aims and aspirations of the International Year of Sustainable Tourism for Development 2017. Through a series of editorial features published throughout this year, Tourism Tattler is profiling African destinations and Africa based tourism products and services who meet and in many cases exceed, sustainable tourism practices in their business operations.

Officially launched at the FITUR International Tourism Fair in Madrid, Spain, on 18 January 2017, the UNWTO International Year of Sustainable Tourism for Development 2017 aims to establish twelve months of global action aimed at advancing sustainable tourism contribution towards the United Nations 2030 Agenda for Sustainable Development.

Speaking at the launch, United Nations Secretary-General, Antonio Guterres, said: "The world can and must harness the power of tourism as we strive to carry out the 2030 Agenda for Sustainable Development. Three of the 17 Sustainable Development Goals (SDGs) include targets that relate to tourism: Goal 8 on promoting growth and decent work, Goal 12 on ensuring sustainable consumption and production, and Goal 14 on conserving marine resources. But tourism also cuts across so many different areas of life and involves so many different economic sectors and socio-cultural currents, that it is connected to the entire Agenda. Beyond the measurable advances that tourism can make possible, it is also a bridge to better mutual understanding among people from all walks of life."

Sustainable Tourism Consumption

The UNWTO has been appointed to lead the 10-Year Framework of Programmes on Sustainable Consumption and Production Patterns (10YFP) Sustainable Tourism Programme (STP) - a collaborative platform to bring together existing initiatives and partnerships and facilitate new projects and activities to accelerate the shift to sustainable consumption and production (SCP) in tourism.

As an implementation mechanism, the vision of the 10YFP STP is for a tourism sector that has globally adopted SCP resulting in enhanced environmental and social outcomes and improved economic performance. *Read more at* www.sdt.unwto.org.

Sustainable Tourism and Climate Change

According to Wikipedia, sustainable tourism is the concept of visiting a place as a tourist and trying to make only a positive impact on the environment, society and economy. Given that without travel there is no tourism, the article cites aviation as being the greatest contributor to tourism's effect on climate change, claiming that 72% of tourism's CO_2 emissions come from transportation, 24% from accommodations, and 4% from local activities.

Sustainable Tourism Guidelines

The Global Sustainable Tourism Council has developed criteria and suggested indicators for Hotels, which aim to provide a common understanding of sustainable tourism and provide a benchmark for the minimum standards that a hotel should aspire to reach. *Download the GSTC Hotel Criteria at* www.gstcouncil.org.

Some of the uses of the criteria include:
- A basis for sustainability certification.
- Guidelines for businesses to become more sustainable, and for businesses to choose sustainable tourism programmes that fulfil these global criteria.
- Provide market access.
- For consumers to identify sound sustainable tourism businesses.
- For media to recognise sustainable tourism providers.
- Help certification bodies to ensure that their standards meet a broadly-accepted baseline.
- Offer governmental, non-governmental, and private sector programmes a starting point for developing sustainable tourism requirements.
- Provide guidelines to education and training bodies.
- Demonstrate leadership that inspires others to act.

The Criteria indicate what *should* be done, not *how* to do it or whether the goal has been achieved. This role is fulfilled by performance indicators, associated educational materials, and access to tools for implementation, all of which are an indispensable complement to the GSTC Criteria.

EDITORIAL
ACCREDITATION

Official Travel Trade Journal and Media Partner to:

The Africa Travel Association (ATA)
Tel: +1 212 447 1357 • Email: info@africatravelassociation.org • Website: www.africatravelassociation.org

ATA is a division of the Corporate Council on Africa (CCA), and a registered non-profit trade association in the USA, with headquarters in Washington, DC and chapters around the world. ATA is dedicated to promoting travel and tourism to Africa and strengthening intra-Africa partnerships. Established in 1975, ATA provides services to both the public and private sectors of the industry.

The African Travel & Tourism Association (Atta)
Tel: +44 20 7937 4408 • Email: info@atta.travel • Website: www.atta.travel

Members in 22 African countries and 37 worldwide use Atta to: Network and collaborate with peers in African tourism; Grow their online presence with a branded profile; Ask and answer specialist questions and give advice; and Attend key industry events.

National Accommodation Association of South Africa (NAA-SA)
Tel: +27 86 186 2272 • Fax: +2786 225 9858 • Website: www.naa-sa.co.za

The NAA-SA is a network of mainly smaller accommodation providers around South Africa – from B&Bs in country towns offering comfortable personal service to luxurious boutique city lodges with those extra special touches – you're sure to find a suitable place, and at the same time feel confident that your stay at an NAA-SA member's establishment will meet your requirements.

Regional Tourism Organisation of Southern Africa (RETOSA)
Tel: +27 11 315 2420/1 • Fax: +27 11 315 2422 • Website: www.retosa.co.za

RETOSA is a Southern African Development Community (SADC) institution responsible for tourism growth and development. RETOSA's aims are to increase tourist arrivals to the region through. RETOSA Member States are Angola, Botswana, DR Congo, Lesotho, Madagascar, Malawi, Mauritius, Mozambique, Namibia, Seychelles, South Africa, Swaziland, Tanzania, Zambia and Zimbabwe.

Southern African Vehicle Rental and Leasing Association (SAVRALA)
Contact: manager@savrala.co.za • Website: www.savrala.co.za

Founded in the 1970's, SAVRALA is the representative voice of Southern Africa's vehicle rental, leasing and fleet management sector. Our members have a combined national footprint with more than 600 branches countrywide. SAVRALA are instrumental in steering industry standards and continuously strive to protect both their members' interests, and those of the public, and are therefore widely respected within corporate and government sectors.

Seychelles Hospitality & Tourism Association (SHTA)
Tel: +248 432 5560 • Fax: +248 422 5718 • Website: www.shta.sc

The Seychelles Hospitality and Tourism Association was created in 2002 when the Seychelles Hotel Association merged with the Seychelles Hotel and Guesthouse Association. SHTA's primary focus is to unite all Seychelles tourism industry stakeholders under one association in order to be better prepared to defend the interest of the industry and its sustainability as the pillar of the country's economy.

International Coalition of Tourism Partners (ICTP)
Website: www.tourismpartners.org
ICTP is a travel and tourism coalition of global destinations committed to Quality Services and Green Growth.

International Institute for Peace through Tourism
Website: www.iipt.org
IIPT is dedicated to fostering tourism initiatives that contribute to international understanding and cooperation.

ITB Asia 2017
Website: www.itb-asia.com
25 to 27 October 2017 Marina Bay Sands®, Singapore.
ITB Asia is the leading B2B travel trade event for the entire Asia-Pacific region.

Tourism, Hotel Investment and Networking Conference 2017
Website: www.thincafrica..com
THINC Africa 2017 takes place in Cape Town, South Africa from 6-7 September.

The Hotel Show Africa 2017
Website: TheHotelShowAfrica.com
Thousands of hospitality professionals from around the world will be at Gallagher Convention Centre in Johannesburg from 25-27 June.

The Safari Awards
Website: www.safariawards.com
Safari Award finalists are amongst the top 3% in Africa and the winners are unquestionably the best.

PAHTC 2017
Website: www.panafricanhealthtourismcongress.com
08-09 June 2017 at the City of uMhlathuze in KwaZulu-Natal, South Africa.
The Pan-African Health Tourism Congress is being staged to address the interests and needs of Health Tourism Stakeholders in Africa.

AWAKENING AFRICA'S HEALTH TOURISM INDUSTRY

The City of uMhlathuze, Proud host of
THE PAN-AFRICAN HEALTH TOURISM CONGRESS

BUSINESS OPPORTUNITY FAIR & EXHIBITION

08-09 June 2017

Umfolozi Hotel Casino Convention Resort
Empangeni, uMhlathuze
KwaZulu-Natal, South Africa

Book your seat!
Tel. +27 11 040 7351-4
registrar@mcgroup.co.za
www.panafricanhealthtourismcongress.com

Tips on GREENING Your Tourism Business

The tourism industry is often subjected to fads and fashions, and businesses struggle to keep up with these rapidly changing requirements – often for naught, because customers quickly move on to the next craze. But environmental friendliness is a trend that is here to stay. People around the world have become very aware of environmental issues in the past decade, and many are looking for ways to reduce their impact on the planet and to live a more sustainable, responsible lifestyle.

Ecotourists also extend this thinking to their holidays. They seek out destinations and businesses that have "green" practices in place, and even those who are not actively interested in the topic will prefer a sustainable establishment over one that is not. So, going green can have a direct impact on your bottom line, not to mention your reputation as a forward-thinking and responsible business.

Greening a business means putting policies in place that ensure efficient, reduced use of resources (like water, electricity and fuel), sustainable practices, community development, environmental protection and awareness. It is a multifaceted discipline that involves everything from building energy-efficient structures to switching off lights and reducing the frequency that laundry is done.

Many business owners are under the misconception that becoming environmentally friendly incurs many costs and is inconvenient – but a clever greening strategy will result in the opposite effect.

Here are some green practices you can put in place quickly and cheaply:

 Reduce your reliance on electricity-guzzling air conditioning by erecting shade netting over windows, adding shutters or planting trees near buildings – these will reduce the heat that comes in.

 Reduce, reuse, recycle. Reduce the amount of packaging and disposable products you use (don't print out digital documents, for example), reuse containers and materials (empty jars make great flower vases, herb pots or stationery organisers), and recycle materials that are more energy intensive to manufacture from scratch (glass, wtin and plastic are good candidates).

 Rethink the way you use transport. If your establishment offers guests transported tours by car, consider whether those could be conducted on foot or bicycle. Your guests may even appreciate being "closer to the ground" and more in touch with their surroundings.

 Source locally instead of purchasing imported goods. Make the most of the products and services available in the area – this not only results in fresher produce, but also makes your offering more customised and local. Tourists these days appreciate more unique, cultural and local experiences, so this can even become a strong marketing point.

 Be water wise. South Africa is largely a dry climate and water is a scarce resource. Plant indigenous flora on your grounds, catch rainwater for watering and cleaning, install water-saving shower, toilet and tap attachments, and avoid drinking water in plastic bottles – it's costly and environmentally unfriendly. Rather provide jugs of fresh water with a slice of cucumber or lemon as a refreshment to guests.

 Cut down on excess services. Guests don't change their sheets and towels every day at home, so they don't need to have these replaced every day. Offer this as an extra service rather than as a basic feature, and explain your reasoning – guests will understand and appreciate that they can make a simple contribution like this.

 Educate your staff and guests about responsible and sustainable practices. Provide a leaflet to guests about some ways they can help protect the local environment – they will appreciate the information and your initiative.

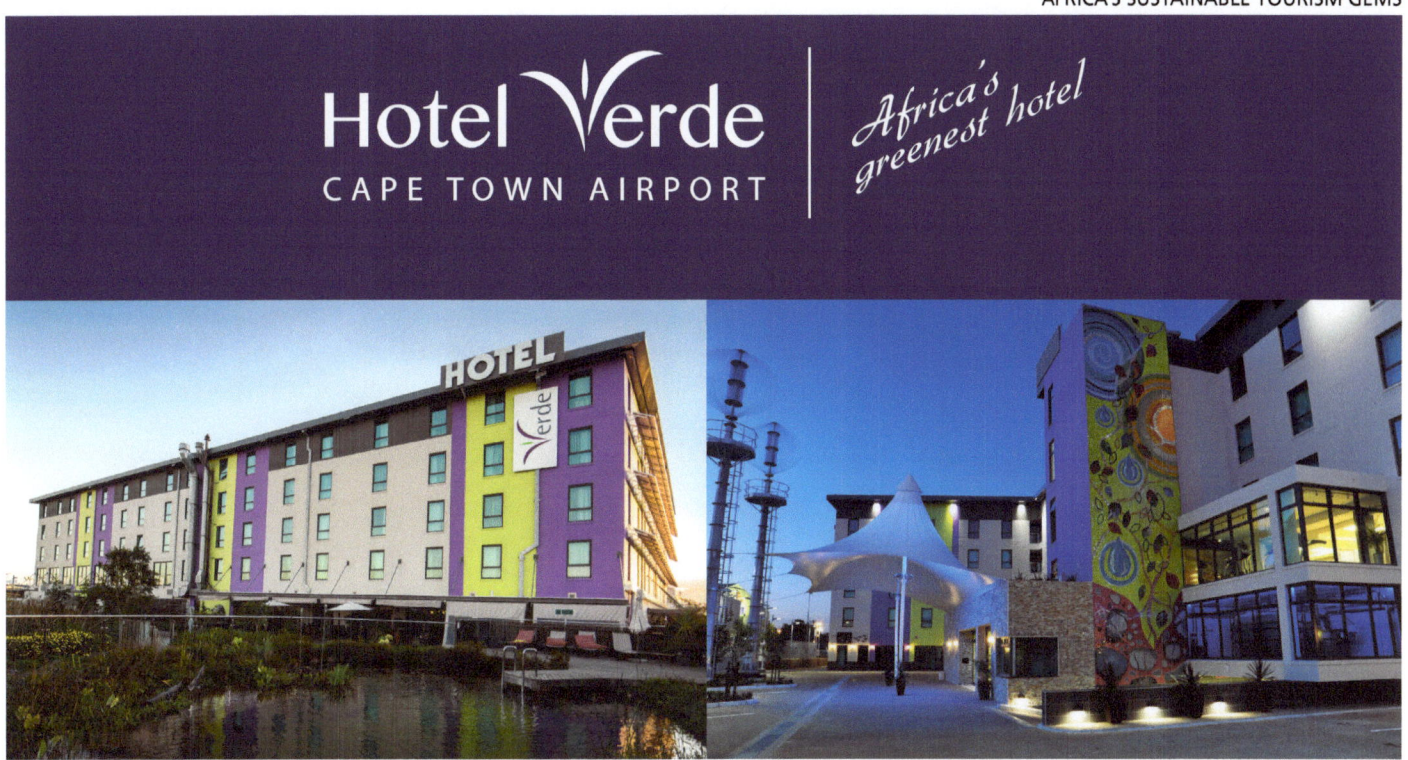

Fair Trade Tourism has partnered with Tourism Tattler in supporting the aims and aspirations of the 2017 International Year of Sustainable Tourism for Development. Through a series of editorial features published throughout this year, Tourism Tattler will be profiling a selection of Fair Trade certified tourism businesses who meet, and in many cases exceed, sustainable tourism practices.

All Fair Trade Tourism certified properties, products and services have met stringent criteria focusing on:
- Fair wages and working conditions
- Fair operations, purchasing and distribution of benefits
- Ethical business practices
- Respect for human rights, culture and the environment.

The Fair Trade Tourism Certified label is the mark of global best practice in sustainable tourism across Africa.

By using Fair Trade certified members, travellers or members of the travel trade, are assured that the tourism business which carries this label has been assessed by an independent, third-party auditor, adheres to the Fair Trade Tourism standard, which is recognised by the Global Sustainable Tourism Council, and is committed to fair, responsible and sustainable tourism.

Selecting a Fair Trade Tourism-certified business also provides assurance that local travel benefits communities and economies as the business is operated ethically in a socially and environmentally responsible manner.

Fair Trade Tourism also recognises like-minded certification programmes in other African countries through mutual recognition agreements with the Seychelles Sustainable Tourism Label; Eco Awards Namibia; Responsible Tourism Tanzania and Botswana's Ecotourism Certification Programme.

As a non-profit organisation, Fair Trade Tourism is considered the leader in sustainable, responsible tourism in Africa. It grows awareness about responsible tourism, assists tourism businesses to operate more sustainably and facilitates the Fair Trade Tourism certification programme in South Africa, Mozambique and Madagascar.

Fair Trade Tourism certification is available for the following categories of tourism businesses:
- Accommodation
- Tourism facilities (such as spas and conferencing),
- Food services (such as restaurants)
- Activities (such as day trips and tours)
- Attractions (such as museums or botanical gardens)
- Volunteer programmes.

View Africa's Sustainable Tourism Gems already listed on the UNWTO IYSTD2017 official website at:
www.tourism4development2017.org

+27 (0)12 342 2945
www.fairtrade.travel

PARTNER SPECIAL FEATURE AFRICA'S SUSTAINABLE TOURISM GEMS

HOME SEARCH · ABOUT · GET INVOLVED · BLOG · CONTACT US | GET LISTED ON ECO ATLAS

Launching Africa's sustainable tourism gems this month with a selection of South Africa's eco-friendly hotels and lodges, Tourism Tattler has partnered with Eco Atlas – an award winning eco-travel choice website. Where a featured eco-friendly property is already listed on Eco Atlas, we've shown the applicable icons.

RESOURCE USE

 **Water Saving:** 3 or more of the following practices in place: a no-leak policy, water audit, flow restrictors on taps and shower heads, dual flush toilet cisterns, harvesting rain water, utilising waste water (grey water), only watering early morning and evening, alien tree removal, planting water wise, drip irrigation system, compost toilet, garden well mulched.

 **Energy Saving:** 3 or more of the following practices in place: energy A-rated appliances, low energy bulbs, geezer blankets and/or timers, established electricity strategy such as switching off appliances and lights when not being used.

 **Recycling:** Established policy to reduce and re-use waste, the recycling of any of the following resources: Paper, Glass, Tin, Plastic and Organic Matter, on-site composting and wormeries.

 **Renewable Energy:** Utilising solar and/or wind energy through solar panels and/or wind turbines.

 **Green Design:** Incorporated into the design of the building: proper insulation, sustainable and renewable building materials, maximising light and energy from the sun, building with recycled materials, non-toxic paints and other building materials, water and energy efficiency.

 **Carbon Neutral:** Planting of trees to off-set the carbon footprint of the establishment and its guests.

EARTH FRIENDLY

 **Eco Cleaning Agents:** utilising or selling products that are fully biodegradable, free of harmful chemicals and not tested on animals.

 **Eco Body Products:** Utilising or selling body products that are fully biodegradable, free of harmful chemicals and not tested on animals.

 **Eco Packaging:** Utilising or selling fully biodegradable packaging and take-away containers made from renewable resources. Accepting returns on product packaging for re-use.

PEOPLE AND EARTH

 **Biodiversity:** no use of pesticides or poisons, planting only indigenous, conservation of indigenous flora and fauna on your property, alien vegetation removal and rehabilitation of indigenous.

 **Local Products:** utilising products grown or manufactured within a 100km radius, the producing or selling of local products.

 **Organic Food:** Utilising or selling food that is produced using a system that sustains the health of soils, ecosystems and people without the use of inputs with adverse effects for biodiversity.

 **Fair Trade:** selling products or implementing policies which contribute to sustainable development by offering better trading conditions to, and securing the rights of, marginalized producers and workers. Registered with Fair Trade Tourism or Fair Trade Label SA.

 **Empowerment:** Skills development, training and profit share programmes which empower staff and enable better working conditions and work opportunities.

ANIMAL FRIENDLY

 **Free Range Chicken:** raised in a humane manner with freedom to roam and constant access to vegetation, fresh air and fresh water. Chickens free of hormones and antibiotics (check with your supplier if they meet all these requirements)

 **Free Range Eggs:** chickens raised in a humane manner with freedom to roam and constant access to vegetation, fresh air and fresh water. Chickens free of hormones and antibiotics (check with your supplier if they meet all these requirements)

 **Badger Friendly Honey:** utilising or selling honey accredited with the Endangered Wildlife Trust certificate to ensure no honey badgers are harmed in the production of the honey.

 **Ethically Farmed Products:** utilising or selling free range meat and/or wool products that are have wildlife friendly management strategies which do not include the trapping, hunting, poisoning and killing of predators. Fair Game endorsed products.

 **Sustainable Fishing:** utilising, promoting or selling sustainable seafood from well managed fisheries as listed in the South African Sustainable Seafood Initiative (SASSI).

 **Free Range Pork:** Raised in a humane manner with freedom to roam outdoors and constant access to vegetation, fresh air and fresh water. Pigs free of hormones and antibiotics and their feed free of animal by-products (check with your supplier if they meet all these requirements)

 **Veg Or Vegan:** Serving purely vegetarian or vegan food, thereby providing healthy eating alternatives and decreasing the amount of natural resources used in the production of food.

SOUTH AFRICA   SPECIAL FEATURE   AFRICA'S SUSTAINABLE TOURISM GEMS

Jaci's Lodges

Jaci's Lodges is the epitome of eco-friendly luxury safaris in South Africa's Big-5 Madikwe Game Reserve. Jaci's promises an authentic, friendly and welcoming safari experience for eco-conscious guests.

Jaci's Lodges takes its commitment to sustainable tourism to heart. Aside from the Jaci's staff trust, which empowers staff with shareholding in the business, Jaci's is involved in a number of conservation and eco-friendly community projects. These include:

- Nature and wildlife conservation (including rhino anti-poaching)
- Community support & upliftment projects
- Use of non-toxic cleaning products and amenities
- Waste reduction (bulk amenities instead of individual packaging)
- Waste recycling (community operated Collect-a-Can project)
- Community employment (staff and delivery of firewood)
- Water Conservation (grey water recycling and towel / linen re-use).

Jaci's Lodges is an ideal destination for honeymoons, intimate weddings, amateur and professional photographers, birding safaris, family getaways and that much needed bush escape!

For more information connect with Jaci's Lodges via the links below.

QUICK LINKS:

✉ reservations@jacislodges.co.za   ☎ +27 (0)83 700 2071
🏠 www.jacislodges.co.za   f @JacisLodges   🐦 @jacislodges
Midikwe   JacisLodges   jacislodges   Jaci's Lodges - Madikwe

---

Hotel Verde Africa's Greenest Hotel

Hotel Verde, situated at the Cape Town International Airport has recently been certified by Fair Trade Tourism - a prestigious accolade for both Hotel Verde and tourism in South Africa, showing leadership in the rapidly growing 'green experience' tourism market.

Hailed as "Africa's Greenest hotel", the multiple award winning Hotel Verde has been set, since opening in 2013, on proving that luxury and sustainability can go hand in hand. The 145-bedroomed hotel earned its spot as one of the most sustainable hotels in the world, after becoming the first hotel world-wide, to receive a double-platinum green building certification.

The Fair Trade certification brings new weight to Hotel Verde's commitment to responsible tourism principles, verifying the sustainable practices of more than just the hotel's design and building operations. The certification was audited extensively by KMPG and focused on aspects such as fair wages and working conditions, fair purchasing and operations, equitable distribution of benefits and respect for human rights, culture and the environment.

Mario and Annemarie Delicio are the owners behind Hotel Verde, who initiated local community 'Eco Outings' to educate school and university students. Dedicated and passionate about sustainability, they have transformed what was initially just a sensible business proposition into a showcase for all to follow.

QUICK LINKS:

✉ info@hotelverde.com   ☎ +27 (0)21 380 5500   🏠 www.hotelverde.com
f @hotelverdect   🐦 @HotelVerde   📷 hotel_verde   ▶ HotelVerde
g+ Hotel Verde   Hotel Verde Cape Town International Airport

Carbon-Neutral Conferencing. Hotel Verde offers eight state-of-the-art conferencing and events venues ideal for productive meetings, workshops, launches and special events. Companies also receive a carbon-offsetting certificate, which can be used for their sustainability reporting, at no extra cost.

AFRICA'S SUSTAINABLE TOURISM GEMS SPECIAL FEATURE SOUTH Africa

Karongwe Portfolio

Karongwe Portfolio consists of six luxury lodges set in the 9000-hectare Karongwe Private Game Reserve, bordering the Makutsi, Lourene, and Greater Makalali game reserves near Tzaneen in South Africa's Limpopo Province.

What sets Karongwe apart from similar properties in the province is its commitment to working hand in hand in uplifting surrounding communities both in terms of employment and wildlife conservation.

The environment is both honoured and preserved, with all six lodges in the reserve having been carefully built around pre-existing trees to secure as small a footprint as possible.

In addition to the close relationship with the local community regarding the awareness of conservation; Karongwe Portfolio places great emphasis on the youth in terms of education. Karongwe's involvement with local schools and an orphanage has been a rewarding experience for all involved.

Furthermore, the Portfolio has embarked on a successful training program for unemployed adults in the area in various departments of the hospitality industry to assist them in gaining the necessary skills to find employment. Karongwe remains dedicated to this fruitful relationship.

Support of local art also plays a significant role, with impressive South African paintings being celebrated on a gallery display wall in the communal area of Becks Safari Lodge.

Karongwe Private Game Reserve has six luxury lodgings; the recently launched Becks Safari Lodge with 8 safari suites and 2 family or couples-oriented suites, Chisomo Safari Camp (which means 'blessings') with 24 en-suite tented rooms, Kuname Lodge with 5 luxury chalets, Kuname Manor House which can accommodate up to six guests, Shiduli Private Game Lodge with 24 suites, and Karongwe River Lodge with 11 spacious air-conditioned suites and en-suite bathrooms.

Community staff are also trained at the Karongwe Portfolio Spa, which uses the heavenly aromas and herbal purity of the unique Thera Naka body range to create a mesmerising and innovative body and sense-soothing safari, replicating the earthy scents and the awe-inspiring wonder of this most profound continent.

Overall, the Karongwe Portfolio meets the sustainable tourism expectations of the most discerning of ecotourists.

Travel. Enjoy. Respect.

QUICK LINKS:

- reservations@karongweportfolio.com
- +27 11 817 5560
- www.karongweportfolio.com
- @KarongwePortfolio
- @KarongweBig5
- Karongwe Portfolio
- Karongwe Portfolio

ATTRACTIONS

How to develop successful TOURISM ROUTES in South Africa

By **Marlien Lourens**.

Some observers describe the notion of 'route development' as the world's best hope to secure sustainability in travel and tourism. The concept of tourism routes refers to an *"initiative to bring together a variety of activities and attractions under a unified theme and thus stimulate entrepreneurial opportunity through the development of ancillary products and services"*. Route tourism is thus a market-driven approach for tourism destination development.

In several parts of the world, the concept of rural trails or heritage routes has been used, particularly in the context of promoting rural tourism. Routes seem to be a particularly good opportunity for the development of less mature areas with high cultural resources that appeal to special interest tourists, who often, not only stay longer, but also spend more to pursue their particular interest. Routes appeal to a great variety of users such as overnight visitors who visit the route as part of a special interest holiday, or day visitors who frequent the route (or part of it) on excursions.

The essential concept of route tourism is simple, namely that of the linking together a series of tourism attractions in order to promote local tourism by encouraging visitors to travel from one location to another.

The development of tourism routes offers opportunities for the formation of local development partnerships. Some of the best and most successful examples of such 'rural routes' are the development of wine or food circuits, which have been widely researched in Europe, North America and Australasia.

In South Africa, considerable activity also surrounds the development of 'route tourism', involving a linkage together of the tourism resources of a number of smaller centres and collectively marketing them as a single tourism destination region. For many South African small towns, route tourism is a vital component of local economic development. The development of wine routes as part of the strong and growing interest in special interest, wine tourism represents one of the most well-known examples.

Tourism is an important economic sector in Africa within more than half of Sub-Saharan Africa countries. The possibilities of tourism are of growing interest to governments and donor organisations in respect of poverty alleviation. Indeed it is regarded significant that the South African Government's Trade and Industry Chamber, through its Fund for Research into Industrial Development, Growth and Equity (FRIDGE) commissioned the development of a strategic plan for routes and community-based tourism in 2005 (ECI Africa, 2006).

Steps to successful route tourism development

At the outset it must be recognised that most destinations involved in route tourism in South Africa are emerging destinations. It is evident that these destinations need guidelines to assist them through their development phases. The developmental phases of routes have been identified as establishment and positioning, growth and maturity, as graphically portrayed in Figure 5.1. The various phases of development as shown in Figure 5.1 are recognised by specific characteristics. Each phase and its characteristics are described below.

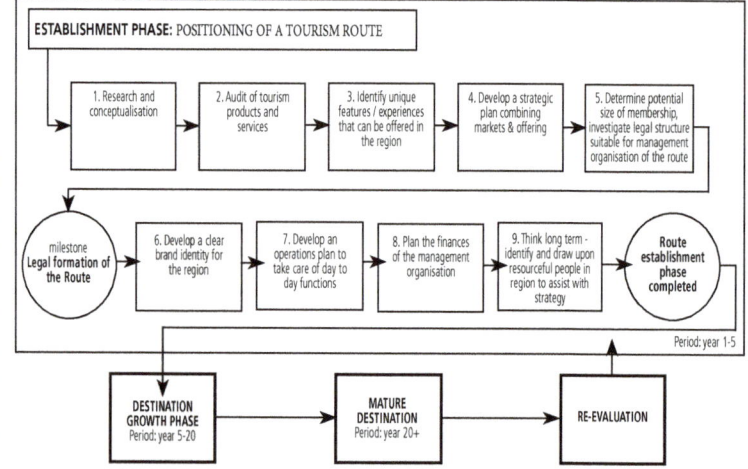

Figure 5.1: Process of Establishing and Positioning of a Route Tourism Destination

When a new route destination is developed, it is usually unrecognised in the market place with only a small number of visitors to the area and limited tourism infrastructure. During this phase committed leadership

14 | Tourism Tattler Trade Journal | MAY 2017

Image courtesy of Mercedes-Benz Commercial Vehicles

is required to see the potential and develop a vision for the region. The establishment and conceptualisation phase of a route as shown in Figure 5.1 contains nine steps, which could take between one and five years to complete. Precision and inclusiveness are required during the establishment and conceptualisation phase to ensure the desired long-term effects.

Firstly, the route must be conceptualised based on solid market research, which identifies key target markets and their requirements. Market research must be conducted on a continuous basis to ensure that the latest tourism trends are included into objectives and strategies for the area. When budgets are tight, it is necessary to align the destination to a local, regional or provincial tourism authority or link to a local university to provide students or volunteers to assist with market research.

Secondly, an audit of tourism products within the designated area must be conducted. This audit may include the natural environment, man-made products and human assets.

Assessments of existing product must be conducted to ensure that products are keeping up to date with the changing dynamics of the tourism industry. The association must clearly determine a minimum standard (equal or higher than the national grading system) for members and a system for regular re-assessment. Failing to set minimum standards, might jeopardise tourist experiences in the area and cause negative marketing which, in the long run, may result in unsuccessful destinations.

Unique selling features

The third step is to scrutinise the tourism assets and identify the unique selling features or experiences of the area and its products. Unique features are extremely important to distinguish and position the destination in the market place. Once the unique selling features have been identified, a macro level strategic plan must be conducted that combines the market requirements and the tourism assets of the region, providing a consolidated approach towards the future development of the area. It is important that the area consults its local, regional and provincial authorities regarding its strategy and future plans for the area. This will ensure that the envisaged route coincides with the macro planning for the region and potentially could link with broader planning or funding initiatives. The next step will be to determine the potential size of the possible membership base.

Tourism products with the ability to complement the unique features and main themes of the route must be lobbied to join the organisation from the early stages. If a legal structure is not yet in place, legal advice must be sought on the best structure suitable for any potential management organisation. Once the organisation is formed, specific portfolios for committee members must be developed according to the identified strategic objectives and to ensure nominated members have the willingness and experience to perform within these portfolios.

Mentorship

It is advisable to incorporate mentorship within the committee and sub-committees or task teams for sustainability of skills. Care must be taken not to incorporate products that are not complementary to tourism or the envisioned branding and values of the area for revenue gain. The association should avoid putting dominant members who act for personal or political gain into management positions. It is also important to be inclusive of all stakeholders within the region to ensure that the benefits are shared by all members of the community.

Further, destination managers should encourage product diversification in the area by putting systems in place to incentivise the correct product mix for the area. For example, it is not healthy for an area to have only accommodation establishments. Accordingly, an association in an area with many accommodation establishments should have high joining fees for products falling within this category.

Research conducted as part of this study shows the importance of unique attractions in a destination and how these products could be used as draw-cards to induce the use of support services. Special events can also be used to produce the same effect.

About the author: Marlien Lourens wrote the content of this article as part of a dissertation document submitted to the University of the Witwatersrand, School of Geography, Archaeology and Environmental Studies in fulfilment of the requirements for a Masters Degree in Tourism in July 2007.

AVIATION

The Vertical Potential Of AIRPORT TRANSFERS

Car hire has long been the go-to ground transport solution for travellers. But with ride-hailing services like Uber and Lyft becoming ubiquitous, it's time we started rethinking the ways in which travellers are getting to and from airports, and the ways in which travel merchants can integrate these into their services.

By **Carey Finn**.

Every year, millions of travellers make their way to and from airports – relying heavily on bus, rail and chauffeured car options to do so. In the Europe and Asia-Pacific regions alone, the number of airline passengers using bus or rail transfers rises to nearly one billion a year – that's a lot of people. It's a lot of potential revenue too. The key question is: when does the traveller start and stop being your customer?

What goes up, must come down… and in the case of travel, it doesn't necessarily stop there. We know that in the corporate travel sphere alone, ground transport has been estimated to represent a full seven percent of spend. It's mostly still sold separately from the rest of the travel arrangements, with passengers required to book directly with the ground transport provider.

There is some logic to this – offering ground transport options in the flight booking flow may impact conversion of the air ticket itself. Rental cars are often offered after the sale, in the form of email prompts and white labels.

But there is room for improvement. We need to see innovation both in the careful integration of ground transport options in the booking flow (timing is everything) and around the product; personalising offers based on customer requirements would be a good start.

A handful of forward-thinking travel service providers have already started to integrate black car and other ground transport options into their offerings: Uber, as we all know, have teamed up with United Airlines, Starwood, the Hilton and Tripadvisor to make journeys easier for travellers; while GroundLink and GroundScope have partnered with Amadeus, Sabre and several other key forces in the industry.

These are just a few of the companies that are working to make the travel experience more inclusive and seamless for customers (Cabforce, Hoppa and Moovit are others on the rapidly growing list) – and this is just the beginning of the industry shake-up. Going forward, we expect to see many more strategic links to fill the gap in the verticals on offer. And it's not going to be limited to chauffeured cars or shuttles, either.

Recently, distribusion.com joined forces with CarTrawler and Amadeus to connect bus operators and travel retailers around the globe via an API-based solution, and they shared some thoughts on the partnership. "The ground transport segment is changing rapidly," noted Pierre Becher, Distribusion's Head of Marketing. "Connecting bus operators and travel retailers on a global scale result in great benefits for all who love to travel."

Becher explained that doing so increases both the transparency and accessibility of bus travel. "It's becoming as easy as booking a flight since bus and airport transfer rides suddenly show up in hundreds of online booking portals or can be booked in thousands of local travel shops. This makes the entire travel experience more convenient."

Convenience – a key consideration for customers

For the travel merchant, it's about more than that though; it's about owning the entire customer travel experience. Integrating ground transport options into the flight booking path means offering customers a one-stop shop for travel arrangements, from their home to their Honolulu hotel, from point A to point B (or even points C and D). This translates to more satisfied travellers, and that leads to increased revenue.

'Partnership' looks set to be the word of the year in the airline industry – it's not just in the area of ground transport that it's having a disruptive impact. We are witnessing innovative collaboration between airlines and OTAs and non-traditional accommodation providers like Airbnb, and there is much, much more to come. It's all about teaming up with companies that are experts in their respective fields to ensure the best service possible for the travel customer. Watch this space for more on that, and other food for thought.

About the author: Carey Finn is a freelance writer for Hepstar - a cutting edge travel-tech company that aims to optimise revenue earned from travel insurance through the use of advanced e-merchandising technology. Should you be interested in learning more about how Hepstar can help you boost ancillary revenue, visit www.hepstar.com.

BUSINESS & FINANCE

Market Intelligence Report

SATSA - Southern Africa Tourism Services Association

Grant Thornton

The information below was extracted from data available as at **03 May 2017**. By Martin Jansen van Vuuren of Grant Thornton.

ARRIVALS

The latest available data from Statistics South Africa is for **January 2017***:

	Current period	Change over same period last year
UK	48 165	4.1%
Germany	33 413	15.4%
USA	23 289	6.9%
India	6 293	-5.2%
China (incl Hong Kong)	12 066	28.3%
Overseas Arrivals	245 074	14%
African Arrivals	794 677	-0.3%
Total Foreign Arrivals	1 040 534	2.8%

HOTEL STATS

The latest available data from STR Global is for **January to February 2017**:

Current period	Average Room Occupancy (ARO)	Average Room Rate (ARR)	Revenue Per Available Room (RevPAR)
All Hotels in SA	63.6%	R 1 360	R 865
All 5-star hotels in SA	68.9%	R 2 565	R 1 768
All 4-star hotels in SA	65.5%	R 1 247	R 817
All 3-star hotels in SA	61.6%	R 962	R 592
Change over same period last year			
All Hotels in SA	-0.7%	7.6%	6.8%
All 5-star hotels in SA	0.3%	7.0%	7.3%
All 4-star hotels in SA	0.5%	7.4%	7.9%
All 3-star hotels in SA	0.7%	4.5%	5.2%

ACSA DATA

The latest available data from ACSA is for **January to March 2017**:

Change over same period last year	Passengers arriving on International Flights	Passengers arriving on Regional Flights	Passengers arriving on Domestic Flights
OR Tambo International	0.9%	-1.4%	-2.0%
Cape Town International	24.9%	0.5%	-1.0%
King Shaka International	8.1%	N/A	1.5%

CAR RENTAL DATA

The latest available data from SAVRALA is for **January to May 2016**:

	Current period	Change over same period last year
Industry Rentals	1 134 620	-1%
Industry Utilisation	74.2%	3.6%
Industry Revenue	2 375 892 450	10%

WHAT THIS MEANS FOR MY BUSINESS

The only updated data available from last month was from ACSA. The ACSA data shows the changing travel patterns of international tourists with less international travellers flying to OR Tambo as direct flights to Cape Town and King Shaka increase. Regional flights from Botswana directly to King Shaka is also in operation. This trend is not only important for tour operators to adjust the tour packages offered but also for car rental companies and even accommodation providers who have transit visitors as a large part of their market.

*Note that African Arrivals plus Overseas Arrivals do not add to Total Foreign Arrivals due to the exclusion of unspecified arrivals, which could not be allocated to either African or Overseas.

For more information contact Martin at Grant Thornton on +27 (0)21 417 8838 or visit: http://www.gt.co.za

BUSINESS & FINANCE

Are South Africa's ROOM RATES Sustainable?

Room rates for South African hotels and lodges increased dramatically between 2016 to 2017, specifically in the 4-star and 5-star markets. Despite the rand having strengthened over the past 12 months, some properties are posting even higher rate increases for 2018, which creates massive problems for booking agents. Are these rate increases sustainable?

By **Des Langkilde**.

Looking at South African hotel room rate increases for 2018, some hotels seem to think that current high occupancy levels are going to last forever.

However, factors that contribute to hotel room rate increases can be complicated, so to simplify the debate and arrive at a logical conclusion, let's take a look at the question from different perspectives.

From an Economics / Currency Perspective

The current high occupancies are really attributable to bookings that were made 12 months ago when the rand was a lot weaker. The recent strength of the rand is a factor that seems to have been completely ignored by properties that have imposed some incredible rate increases.

From a booking agent's perspective, this creates a massive problem as they not only have to contend with room rate increases but with foreign currency exchange rate fluctuations as well.

Based on average room rate increases from 2016 to 2017, a typical R5,000 room in 2016 has increased to R5,900 in 2017.

But how do these room rate increases and currency fluctuations translate in terms of foreign visitors? For the same room, UK, USA and European visitors would have paid:

- UK visitor: approximately £227 in 2016 and £347 in 2017,
- USA visitor: approximately $312 in 2016 and $437 in 2017,
- European visitor: approximately €303 in 2016 and €437 in 2017.

From a Hotel Statistics Perspective

According to STR, formerly known as Smith Travel Research – an American company that tracks supply and demand data for the global hotel industry – hotel performance for Q1 2017 saw occupancy levels rise 5% to 56%, ADR increase 9.8% to $111.15 and RevPAR increased 15.3% to $62.19 across the African continent. In stark contrast, the Middle East reported year-on-year performance declines in the first quarter of 2017. Occupancy fell 1.4% to 70.5%, ADR dropped 6.8% to $173.06 and RevPAR decreased 8.2% to $122.07.

In South Africa, average room occupancy (ARO) levels increased by 8% for all hotel star grades over the past five years (2012-2016), while room occupancy has remained reasonably consistent at an average of 62.6%. Average room rates (ARR) over the same period increased by close to 25%, while revenue per available room (RevPar) increased by nearly 31%. The biggest hotel room rate increases came from the 5-Star sector at 27.3% with average revenue increasing from R917 to R1432 per available room – an increase of 36%.

Looking to the future of hotel rates, Martin van Vuuren, Strategic Development & Planning Director at Grant Thornton says "Growth in average room rates in South Africa over the past five years has been driven by increased demand (particularly from the international market) and a limited increase in the supply of hotel rooms. I expect that this trend will slow in the next five years with growth in the international market slowing to a global average of around 5% with the opening of new hotels currently under construction absorbing some of this growth. Changes in the exchange rate may result in short-term fluctuations but the long term trend should still hold."

From an Agents Perspective

Travel Agents, DMCs and Tour Operators deal with a wide variety of accommodation types and are in tune with rate increases and the impact

BUSINESS & FINANCE

that these have on hotel bookings. Compounding the rates issue for agents is that many hotels are imposing unrealistic cancellation and payment/deposit policies – but that's another story.

Illana Clayton, CEO of TravelSmartCrew* with an annual spend of R1.6 billion in South and Southern Africa in 2016, says: "There is no single factor that impacts on inbound demand. We have seen an exceptionally strong 18 months, attributable to a number of positive contributing factors. Even with a weak exchange rate, South African hotel prices generally are no longer cheap, and many of the tariffs we are seeing now are definitely unsustainable. In a strong demand environment, the temptation to apply large increases is a risky consideration if a long term trade-partnered strategy is desired.

"First support from DMC's and Tour Operators is to the more realistically priced product, and only when those offerings are full, are the higher priced products sold. When demand drops or available stock of rooms increases (i.e. Cape Town in 2018), those who have had a more realistic and long-term view on sustainable rate increases will reap the benefit. We are still seeing some ZAR accommodation units applying 20-50% increases for 2018, while many USD based product in Southern Africa are either decreasing their rates or holding them for 2018. We are in for an interesting 2018."

From an Owner's Perspective

And last, but certainly not least, the perspective of an accommodation property owner is important to consider seeing as the buck stops here and what better place to ask for an opinion than a safari lodge.

Vernon Wait, Marketing Director at Lalibela Private Game Reserve says: "Whilst Lalibela has enjoyed an absolutely bumper 2016 and the first quarter of 2017, we have looked at the macroeconomic environment when deciding on our rates for 2018. The recent strength of the rand weighed very heavily on our decision and we have taken the view to hold rates for 2018 steady. The new owners feel very strongly that this is a long-term project that requires long-term relationships with suppliers.

"Even with us holding rates steady 2018, we are mindful that in USD, Euro and UK pound terms it will cost more to send clients to Lalibela in 2018. A rate increase for 2018 was simply not an option," concludes Wait. *(Read more on 'The Role of Tour Operators in Safari Bookings' here).*

Conclusion

According to leading industry experts then, it would seem that South African hotels should take the lead shown by Lalibela and by USD based hotels in neighbouring countries and adopt a cautious approach to room rate increases, looking for long-term sustainability in terms of room occupancy levels and RevPar, specifically over the next five years.

Anecdotal evidence certainly shows that some (not all) properties have posted massive increases for 2018 – some as high as 45% but with 20% increases not being at all uncommon. With no-one knowing what's going to happen to the rand, there is a serious risk that South Africa is in the process of out-pricing itself relative to other markets.

---

*TravelSmartCrew shareholders include African Pride Tours, Africapass, Africa Travel Group, Cedarberg African Travel, Egoli African Destinations, Giltedge Travel, Highline Tours & Travel, Ilanga Travel, Inspirations ITT, Pembury Tours, Personal Africa, Safari365, Southern Destinations, SW Africa, Tour d'Afrique and XO Africa.

DESTINATIONS

SPONSORED FEATURE

RÉUNION ISLAND

In the meetings industry, no other destination has such an apt name as Île de la Réunion (The meeting Island). This tropical island is actually one of the French overseas departments and is a popular destination for exotic incentives with European quality guaranteed.

In many ways, Reunion Island resembles Hawaii, except of course for being French and lying in the Indian Ocean to the east of Madagascar. It lies on a volcanic hot spot, which partly explains the wonderful abundance of flora. Throughout the year, Reunion has a tropical climate tempered by the ocean and trade winds with temperatures between 20°C and 30°C.

The possibilities are endless on this natural Indian Ocean Island. From the blue lagoon to the rocky cliff sides, the coastline allows for a lot of water sports and other water related activities: swimming, deep sea diving and fishing or simply lying on the beach and watching the sun go down. Hiking-fans will enjoy exploring the island's mountain range and nature reserves.

Reunion Island has succeeded in preserving this exceptional natural beauty with more than 40% of the island classified as a nature reserve. In fact, the volcanic mountain peaks, ramparts and cirques have received UNESCO World Heritage status.

Long before the island became a quality meetings destination, it was already a meeting point for European, African, Indian and Chinese cultures. Thus, events, festivals, architecture, gastronomy and more have evolved into a warm, festive and spicy mix, perhaps best represented by the warm welcome of the Creole inhabitants.

Reunion Island guarantees the same levels of comfort and standard of living as you would expect from a European destination. High level of hygiene and healthcare. No need for any vaccinations, it is malaria free, offers state of the art communication technology, and all this in a completely safe and secure environment.

Reunion Island is visa free for South African passport holders, which is a great advantage for incentives and meetings, and it is only a 4 hour flight from Johannesburg (3 x weekly) on Air Austral.

The hotels on offer in Reunion are as varied in styles and locations as they are alike in their hospitality. They can be found in the charming towns, tourist hotspots or in coastal pleasure centres. Private tennis courts, swimming pools, and other facilities are commonly available. All hotels on the island are up to European standards.

Reunion Island is ideal for incentive and team building.

DESTINATIONS

Tropical INCENTIVE with a French Touch

Image credit: Frog974 Photographies

Image credit: Gabriel Barathieu

Image credit: Emmanuel Virin

Image credit: Laurent Bèche

REUNION ISLAND
THE ULTIMATE EXPERIENCE

Réunion Island Tourism Board is represented by Atout France in South Africa.

CONTACTS:

 +27 010 205 0201

 reunionisland.za@atout-france.fr

 GotoReunionSA

 @reuniontourisme

 @reuniontourisme

 blog.welcometoreunionisland.com

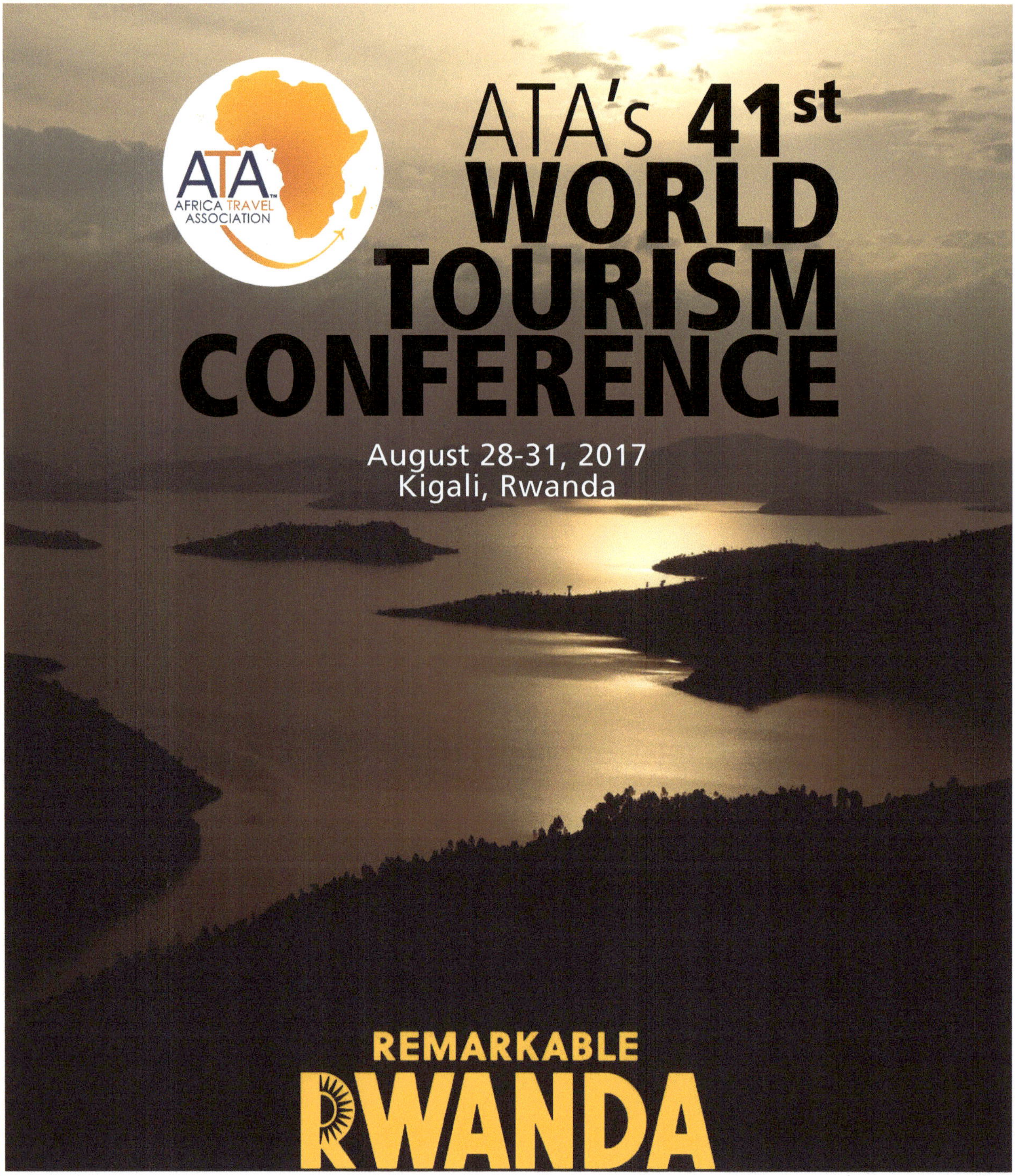

http://conference.africatravelassociation.org/

CORPORATE COUNCIL ON AFRICA

RDB | RWANDA DEVELOPMENT BOARD

Register Now - Click Here

tourism TATTLER
News, Views, and Reviews for Travel in, to and out of Africa

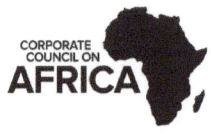

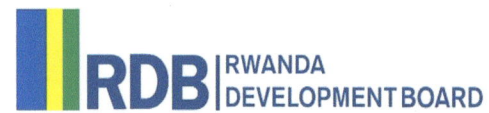

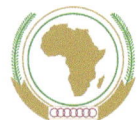

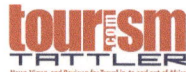

MEDICAL TOURISM CERTIFICATION
Added Value Or Waste Of Money?

By **Angeliki Katsapi**.

The medical tourism and tourism medicine market is an increasing but also challenging market. Patients have particular needs when undergoing treatment abroad. Pre-, on-site- and post-treatment take place in different countries and need to be managed to assure high quality and cost-effective medical care during all phases of the treatment process.

The medical service structure and the operational and quality levels differ among countries depending on each country's living standards, current regulatory, financial and organisational conditions. Moreover, quality is always relative due to the individual perception and culture and also due to the scientific or professional standards that are implemented.

Furthermore, difficulties in international patient management arise as a result of cultural differences, language barriers but also legal issues, a different understanding of medicine or an interruption of cross-border procedures, for example, in the frame of the provision of reliable information and documentation in the pre-treatment stage.

The processes and procedures associated with the treatment of international patients need to be defined, implemented and realised in the frame of the healthcare facility's Total Quality Management System (TQMS).

General hospital accreditation systems are an excellent basis for the facility's quality management but do not cover the quality criteria and respective management needed to map the international patient care cycle and associated processes e.g. before and after the treatment onsite.

Proper management of international medical tourist services as demanded by specialised medical tourism certification programs can bridge the gap between the international patients' demands and the hospital's requirements for the provision of these services. At the end, both sides will benefit by achieving their objectives.

The Pan-African Health Tourism Congress is scheduled to take place from 7-9 June at the Umfolozi Hotel Casino Convention Resort, Empangeni, KwaZulu-Natal. Aside from acting as catalysts for Health Tourism development while addressing 'brain regain' amongst other important issues, the idea for the Pan-African Health Tourism Congress was to serve as a motivator and catalyst:

- For continent-wide Health Tourism development
- To prompt African governments to improve the quality of services at public sector facilities
- To help incentivize health sector professionals of the African diaspora to return home and capitalise on the opportunities opening up for the development of Health Tourism.

For more information visit the PAHTC2017 website at www.panafricanhealthtourismcongress.com, or contact Ashley Santos on +27 (0)11 436 9014, or email her at ashley@mcgroup.co.za. Join the conversation on Twitter @PAHTC2017

About the author: Ms Angeliki Katsapi is an internationally active certified auditor for quality and safety management systems in healthcare and medical tourism services. She is an assessor for Temos International and the Managing Director of Temos Hellas.

MARKETING

Protecting the Female Traveller

Since the inception of modern tourism women have played a significant role in the development of the world's largest composite industry.
By **Dr Peter Tarlow.**

The tourism industry is proud of the fact that as one of the world's newest industries, women have played a profound role in tourism's success. One only needs to attend a travel industry conference to note that women not only form a significant proportion of those in attendance, but are also often in the majority. Women hold top CEO positions throughout the industry, to the point that no one in the travel industry gives a second thought to a person's gender. In the world of travel agencies, the great majority are women, and women are often not merely travel agents but also the agencies' owners.

That is not to say that women have not been exploited. Women in most of the developing world often do not have the same gender-bias free opportunities as they do in the more developed nations. Gender equality, however is not equally distributed. Thus, while in some countries women have not moved beyond menial tasks in other nations such as Guatemala, Belize, and Tanzania women have made significant progress and are on par with their sisters in the more developed world.

In many nations around the world women hold cabinet level positions in tourism and head their nation's tourism industry. Women not only play a significant role in the travel industry but as more and more women have entered into the work-force, women form an important segment of the travelling public. The term 'single woman traveller' does not refer to a woman's marital status but rather to the fact that she is travelling alone, be that trip for reasons of pleasure or business. Because women are now such an important part of the travel industry, they demand and receive specific travel amenities. Successful travel and tourism businesses, take into account specific female security needs. Here are some ideas to consider for improving the security of your tourism entity or community for the 'single' female traveller.

- **Fair game?** The world is not always fair to women. Although blatantly sexist and unfair in many parts of the world, a woman travelling by herself is considered to be 'fair game.' The first rule of thumb then is to know the culture to which you are travelling. If the culture tolerates 'sexual harassment' then do everything possible to avoid single travel. Even in highly sensitised countries women should use extra precautions.
- **Know your security strengths and weaknesses.** Never begin to think of any form of security without first doing a clear analysis. Go through your locale and develop lists of what might be a special danger to female guests. While many women are good at spotting danger, it is not their responsibility to know each and every danger spot; instead it is the host community or business that needs to pay extra attention to female security needs.
- **Educate your staff and then educate some more!** Your security is only as good as the people who work not only in security but on the front lines. Take the time to speak with all front line personnel about women's security issues. Make sure they are sensitive to the special needs of women travelling alone and know how to give good and correct advice.
- **Use social networks.** Seek out networks that serve the travelling woman. Many of these networks can provide up to the minute advice. A quick search of the web provides a wealth of information regarding women's travel networks.

When educating your staff and/or guests about women's travel safety, consider some of the following points:

* At hotels, help female guests to avoid ground-floor rooms. These are the rooms to which it is easiest for a potential attacker to gain access. Instead seek the third or fourth floor, and in sight of the elevator.
* Always carry a flashlight. It is amazing how a flashlight may scare off a potential assailant.
* If your car breaks down do not stay in it alone. You are safer on foot than locked in a car that cannot move.
* A woman should never walk alone on poorly lit paths, close to bushes or in places where you cannot be seen, this rule of security is as valid in the day as it is in the night.
* Remember that while all women may be subjected to rape drugs, this is especially true of any woman travelling in a country that is not her own. Be careful whom you drink with, what you drink and into whose vehicle you enter.
* Make sure that someone knows who you are, and where you are, and never forget that there are those who see a single woman as a prime candidate for sexual assault.
* When travelling abroad, even for purposes of business, dress according to the dictates of the host culture. While it is not fair to victimise a woman due to the way she may choose to dress, the fact is that in some cultures a woman is blamed for being assaulted simply due to the dress code that she chooses to follow.
* Watch your purse/bag at all times. Purse-snatchers and other crimes of distraction artists often seek out single women travellers and assume that women are easier targets then are men. Often purse-snatchers prefer crowded areas. Always stay alert in places like bus stations and during street celebrations, where you are likely to be jostled - thieves use these circumstances to grab purses, handbags and briefcases from women travellers.
* If someone does snatch your purse, let it go. If it is not a matter of life or death, then you are probably better off simply losing the item. If it is a matter of life and death, scream, run and hit the attacker where it will hurt the most.

About the author: Dr. Peter E. Tarlow is the author of "Tourism Tidbits," a regular newsletter from the USA. To subscribe send an email to ptarlow@tourismandmore.com

MARKETING

The Hidden Power of Ritual

The priceless power of rituals in travel experiences must be taken into account in marketing. By **Anita Mendiratta**.

Walking down the busy street in Hanoi, a day of meetings over and a quiet night in the hotel ahead, he slowed his pace to be able to take in the here and now. The distance between the office and hotel was too close for a taxi, and the streets too alive with that wonderful colour and chaos to simply rush past. He also wanted to make sure that he did not leave without fulfilling the one last thing he had on his personal 'to do' list. He had to find a local craft shop, he had to find a Buddha.

For as long as he had been travelling to Asia, wherever he went, he would take home a Buddha statue. For one of his colleagues, it was cufflinks, that was the preferred collectable. For him, it was Buddhas, which was interesting as he wasn't even a formal follower of the faith. His apartment back home had become home to a collection of Buddhas – bronze, marble, wood, jade, sandstone, large and small, made of materials from all across Asia. Each piece not only brought an artistic richness to his home, it reminded him of where he had been, even if just for a few days, making that time and place more real, giving it personal meaning and connection.

It was his ritual, the one thing he did for himself while he was busy doing business for his company.

RITUALS

We all have them. We all perform them in one way or another, whether we actively recognize them or not. They are more than just habits - repetitive actions done instinctively and often subconsciously. Instead, rituals are moments that add heightened meaning and memory to what could otherwise be a series of seconds that pass unacknowledged. For travellers, people constantly on the move and constantly entering places of change, rituals provide an important rhythm to life in transit. They create a sense of control, of balance, or of connection to a time and place. However defined and however performed, rituals can be powerful influences on who we are, where we are, and what becomes important to us.

> **Rituals** are anticipated, undertaken with care, and celebrated with a simple private smile when complete. They are a part of who we are. And often, they add to the definition of how we live our lives.

A ritual may be as simple as waiting until on the plane, glass of champagne in hand, before leaving an '*out of country on business*' voicemail on one's mobile phone to let callers know to text or email instead of leaving a voice message. The ritual may simply be placing one's personal reading by the bedside table as soon as entering a new hotel room so that a feeling of '*this is my place*' can be created. Or it may be collecting artefacts of a certain theme while travelling. Rituals encourage us to pause, be still, mark the moment, and embed the memory. Importantly, they allow us to connect with a time and place, especially when the ritual is performed not just by us, but on us.

RITUALS IN TOURISM

Travel and tourism, while an industry reliant on essential hardware – buildings, hotel rooms and facilities, convention centres, airports, aircraft – has become increasingly dependent on the software for customer attraction, retention, and ambassadorship. They also become an element of competitive differentiation.

Rituals embedded in the travel experience offer brands – airlines, hotels, attractions – the ability to make a meaningful, personal connection with travellers.

EMBEDDING RITUALS WITHIN THE EXPERIENCE

Interestingly, rituals, while an investment in guest experience and brand identity, need not even cost a penny. Simple ceremonies, inspired moments of pause, and even stimulation of a sense, can be all that is required to embed a ritual in the mind and heart of the traveller.

Examples of such simple yet impactful rituals include:

- **Six Senses Sanctuary in Phuket:** inviting guests to make a wish and strike a massive, hanging Asian Gong on both arrival and departure from the island, feeling the deep sound and vibrations of the gong as they set the tone for the guest's wellness visit, and its enduring impact.
- **Air Tahiti Nui:** during flights to Tahiti, the airline distributes tiny white Tiare flower buds, the island nation's national flower, seeding the scent in the minds and memories of travellers, offering a fragrant embrace of 'welcome' to first-time visitors and 'welcome home' to those returning... and creating an aromatic connection to Tahiti and her islands wherever in the world that traveller encounters that scent in the future.
- **Doubletree Hotels:** since the 1980s, Doubletree Chocolate Chip Cookies have become a signature part of guest check-in, given to guests warm and deliciously gooey. Offered in more than 200 hotels and resorts worldwide, at present 30,000 cookies are given to guests every day of the week - more than 10,950,000 every year.

CREATE YOUR OWN RITUAL

When seen as an investment, the value of rituals is priceless.

Importantly, each and every destination, property, and attraction in the world has the ability to create a single, signature ritual that can act as a powerful part of the brand's DNA and delivery. Taking the time and care to identify the right ritual, based on the:

- brand proposition;
- local culture and conscience;
- uniqueness and appropriateness;
- guest (motivation for visitation and mindset during the visit, not just demo/geo/psycho make-up);
- situation during the visitor experience; and
- desired impact is, also, an investment in the business.

That investment, however, must be maintained for it to be embedded and owned by the brand. Removing the ritual, or simply missing one occasion, can make the traveller feel something is wrong, something is missing, or worst – someone is cost cutting.

Whatever the act, whatever the item, rituals make lasting connections to places visited, for work or for play. It is not about the product, the price, or the performance – it is about the spirit of the moment and its enduring meaning.

MARKETING

All You Need to Know About
EMAIL MARKETING

Email Marketing is one of the best advertising sales tools around. You could say that it is the pipeline through which sales reach your business, easily returning R500 to every R12.50 you spend. Integrate this with social networks and the return is even higher.

Where to start!

The first tool that you will need is a bulk email host. Your normal email client (probably the provider who hosts your website) will have restrictions on the number of emails that you can send per day. If you abuse this threshold your email address (and your website domain) will be 'blacklisted' – a term that tells email blocking programs that your email is 'unsafe' or 'spam' and prevents it from appearing in a subscriber's inbox.

Bulk email hosting services such as MailChimp and MailerLite are free for mailing lists of up to 1000 recipients and have affordable monthly options as your subscriber list grows over time. Both have some great features that make creating email campaigns simple, like free design templates with 'drag & drop' functionality, rich text editing and built-in photo editing. More importantly, both have really good list management tools to keep track of your email campaign performance and to manage and protect the integrity of your mailing list.

The Message

As far as the message is concerned, you are trying to generate more value for your customers, which in turn generates more sales.

So the first thing you have to do is NOT to start writing a newsletter.

What you have to do is determine what your main strategy (your personal angle) is going to be.

There are two parts of communications that you have to work out at the start, one is who are my sales prospects exactly (e.g. holiday, business travellers, or travel and hospitality colleagues), in other words, what are their personalities, and secondly how do I communicate my company's brand and products to them.

Sounds easy? Well, it isn't, but there is an easy way to find out.

The first thing you do when you have the power of email marketing at hand, assuming you have a customer mailing list that is up to date and you can segment the different types of customers, is to send them an email. This is really a survey to find out what your customers think about your company's destinations, its services, your colleagues, and you. After all, It's about what impressions they have. Impressions translate into values, and it's those values that form the basis of your communication with them. Key is to know exactly how your clients like you to communicate with them. You can do this by setting up a simple and effective survey letter.

First of all, you need to place yourself in your client's situation and a good introduction paves the way to getting good answers back. Above all Keep it simple! So perhaps this message to travellers will suit:

Subject: Thank you from South Africa

Dear (Name)

I trust that you had a pleasant trip to your onward destination and hope that your stay with us was a happy and memorable one.

As a valued guest, your opinion is very important to us and I would like to ask your opinion on the following questions, which may help us to improve our service to you in the future:

What is your impression of our accommodation?

What is your impression of our food?

What is your impression of our staff?

What kind of atmosphere would you say we create?

I am grateful for your answers. Please don't hesitate to criticise as it is only by knowing our weaknesses that we can build on our strengths.

Please visit our website or follow us on social media to keep abreast of changes as we implement your feedback

We at (your company name) look forward to hosting you again.

Kind Regards,

Your name

(insert signature / contact details)

EMAIL MARKETING 101

Response handling using autoresponders

Now that you have hit the send button your email is on its merry way, and there is no telling what the response might be. Have I checked for any eventualities you might think? Well here is how to prepare for that.

In the email marketing application, you set up your first autoresponder. An autoresponder is really another email that you create which is sent out when a certain condition or a number of conditions are met. For example, if a certain number of recipients haven't responded to your first email within a number of days. In this event, the autoresponder email can be scheduled to be sent out to those recipients that didn't answer within the specified time limit.

Newsletter Content

Most of the newsletters I get in my inbox are from safari companies or DMCs, generally informative on the product level telling me what location, what activities and what accommodation they provide plus who to contact and how to get there.

So what's wrong with that? Nice email from nice people - what exactly am I missing here?

First of all, I like getting newsletters from people in the travel trade and often look to just see what it is they are doing, but as soon as I see yet another "Look at my product" message I quickly click away. We all get messages like this every day and they are basically all the same, churning out the same information over and over again. You really can't tell these newsletters apart unless they have been templated in which case that might have a pleasing effect after all.

So how does one go about producing an effective newsletter?

Let's first go back to some essentials. For instance, what is important in sending out a monthly newsletter? Is it the product you want to show or is it what your subscribers want to read? We often forget to dig into the personas at the other end of our virtual pens to find out what they value the most. It is so easy to slip back into the old information bashing routine. So let's get under the hood with some simple specifics.

Every successful newsletter does the following:
- takes the customer on a short but interesting journey,
- shows product information and
- illustrates the combination of both magnificently.

These points are absolutely key to creating lasting relationships and of course trust. I know it's easy to say; "Hey this is what we are going to do!" and then leave out the important stuff, so what exactly lies at the heart of a good relationship bonding newsletter? Well, it is most importantly 'INVOLVEMENT'.

What every subscriber really wants to know

What every subscriber wants to know and doesn't ask is:

'HOW INVOLVED ARE YOU WITH YOUR PRODUCT'.

Aha! So how do you show subscribers how involved you are? Well, quite simply by giving them a view of your actions, your drive, and your imagination. What readers really want is to know you, your colleagues, what happens in your office or out in the bush, how certain things were achieved, how you or your colleagues coped with a difficult situation, you name it - any personal anecdotes together with a healthy dose of humour. Humour always works in forging relationships (even if you are an undertaker).

That's it?

No, it isn't, now comes the fun part - merging your anecdotes and your product information together. This takes a bit of imagination, for example, what anecdote can you tell that has something to do with the product you are selling? Ask your colleagues, your family and your friends. You'll come up with something guaranteed.

Last but not least

The header (tagline) of your newsletter is important, so make sure it rings a bell with your subscribers! Make sure your branding and newsletter design is personally targeted to the market and subscriber base you are communicating with.

Newsletter Design

All of your good intentions and valuable content can be wasted if you don't pay attention to how that content is managed and distributed. There are some highly important guidelines to remember and work towards if you are going to make your email campaign succeed.

Your email address and subject line.

Your email address and subject line is the first information people will see when mail arrives in their in-box. On average readers spend 3 to 4 seconds deciding if your email is worth reading or not. With professionals getting many emails a day there is no guarantee that people will view what you send. It's important that they recognise you instantly as a trustworthy and recognisable source, so forget about using info@ or such, instead use a personal email address. Your subject line is your make or break line, 50 characters stand between you and the trash-bin, so make sure this stands out visually and offers interest from the word go. Use your reader's favourite product name with a consistent repetitive identifier, make creative use of brackets and try out different variations of capitalization! Gmail Outlook and Iphone also offer 100 characters or less of preview text next to the subject line. These snippets are pulled from the first lines of text in your email, so offer something valuable here and/or include a call to action. Use timely topics and urgency. Make three different variants and send each test email to a segment of your subscribers (don't forget to include yourself in the list). Determine if your email looks spammy next to other messages. Decide to use the most successful one for the rest of your campaign and continue to repeat and improve your formula from here on.

Your message, is it going to work?

The first thing a large percentage of viewers won't see are the images contained in your email.

Most readers are asked if they would like to click to see the images. 67% of desktop, 100% of web-mail and 80% of mobile email clients block images by default. The best way to deal with this and to help readers to decide to view your email is to make use of alt texts, captions and tabled colour blocks.

If you are painstakingly collecting first, second, and surnames for only email marketing purposes you need to know that making use of your subscriber's first name or surname does not significantly improve opening or reading rates. Also on the data collecting side it is easier to let newsletter subscribers just enter their first and second name in one text field instead of separating them into two

EMAIL MARKETING 101

fields. Video, Flash, rollovers, JavaScript and background images don't work as they do in the browser. Outlook doesn't display backgrounds by default, so make creative use of background colours instead. Different email clients also display content differently, so it's important to give specific formatting values (even if that value is 0) to each individual element especially tables (cell padding and cell spacing) also image borders. Make sure to use web-safe fonts like arial, verdana, trebuchet and georgia otherwise your readers may have trouble viewing your text.

Matching content with design
Now that you have safeguarded your design and created successful solutions for the email being read by readers, let's concentrate on the message and product specifics.

Prioritise
Try to prioritise your message topics, products and activities. Determine your main product (your bestsellers or seasonal offer) and package this as a luxury offer. In design terms give that product it's own full size block with clear call to action button. Package your activities in three smaller blocks with read more links to your website landing pages. Offer more products (packages) each with their own urgency and call to action links. Give readers clear choices, never try to display something that you cannot describe clearly and directly.

Textual content
Make use of questions in your text (even in topic headers), people always like to be asked to do something. Try to visualise what the top priority in your reader's minds is and use this with clear calls to action (but don't exaggerate). Mix your storyline as best you can with your product offer and look real and convincing (be you!).

Choosing a design
When choosing a design ask yourself the following:
1. Is there enough space for my logo and top banner, it is important to display these in the right proportions.
2. How many columns do I want (using columns usually means a shorter length email as product offers can be displayed effectively alongside). This depends on whether you are going to employ a right hand margin for your offers and/or individual products separated alongside.
3. Does the design (colours, font, layout) match with my audience's inspirations- expectations: technical, romantic, active, cultural.
4. Are the social buttons positioned in the right place (in the footer, underneath the content)
5. Is it easy to alter the design to my liking? (some designs are hard to manipulate due to design constrictions in the code)

Remember
The landing pages that the email is linked to must be consistent with the content in the email, otherwise this will frustrate readers and result in your emails being read by a shrinking audience over time.

Winning formula
Once you have created a successful format, stick to it, however always keep an open mind to new developments that your readers are sensitive to. This in turn will help you to develop trustworthy relationships and in future exponentially grow your mailing lists.

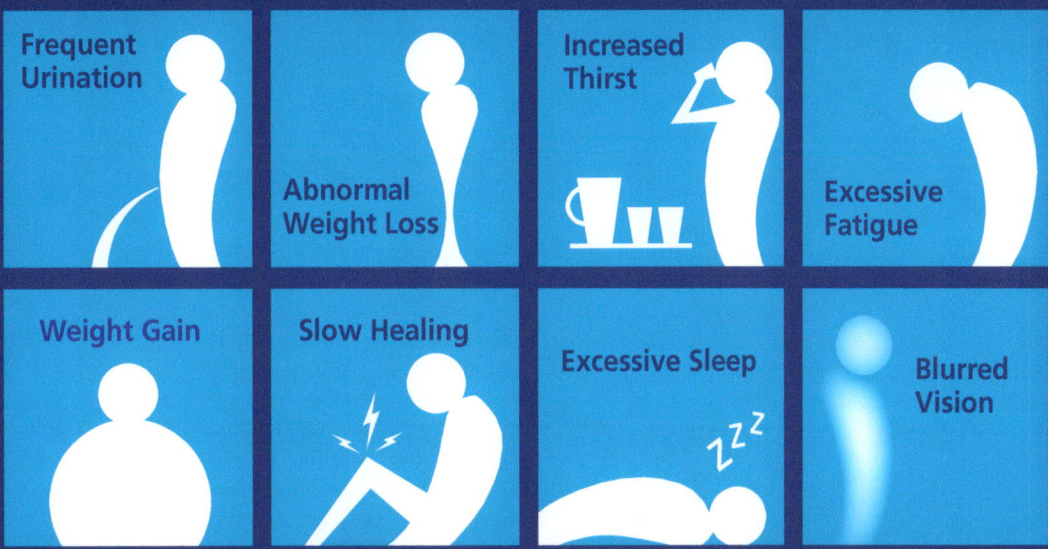

A guide to Cultural Tourism

Cultural tourism, or culture tourism as it is sometimes called, is a type of niche tourism that attempts to represent the stories and lifestyles of the people from the past and in the present authentically. As such, it places particular focus on art, architecture, religion, food, clothing and anything else that may have contributed to shaping a group of people's way of life, writes **Yvonne Nhuta** of GetSmarter.

This kind of tourism normally occurs in urban areas with particular historical significance or cultural facilities, such as museums and theatres. Cultural tourism also highlights the various traditions of indigenous communities through observing their rituals, customs as well as their values and lifestyle. Tourism therefore serves as the carrier of culture and cultural tourism has become the platform for cultural consumption.

As a powerful tool for economic development, tourism is responsible for jobs, providing new business opportunities and strengthening local economies. When cultural tourism is done effectively it can aid in securing an area's natural and cultural resources, while improving the quality of life for residents and visitors. One of the main ideas behind this kind of niche tourism is that people should be able to save their heritage and culture while sharing it with visitors and reaping the economic benefits of tourism.

Getting started

Ideally, most regions engaging in cultural tourism can benefit greatly from it. New businesses, more jobs and higher property values are just some of the advantages of investing in cultural tourism. Getting a handle on this type of tourism will require initially contemplating the availability of resources such as arts organisations, festival organisers and arts venues which can be used in attracting visitors. Some of the things you will need to consider include your location, timing, the potential visitor profile, what the tourists want to see and exactly what you want to achieve.

Once you have pooled together all your resources, you can establish what sorts of attractions your area is prepared to offer potential tourists. This can range from art festivals to museum showcases depending on how wide and how solid your area's resources are. Then, you need to ensure that you have advertised the event or site, leaving enough time for potential tourists to plan their visits. Peak times include major seasonal holidays and periods that coincide with other national events.

As the number of people coming and going out of the region will increase, there will be increased demands on the infrastructure. Consequently, before attracting visitors, the roads, airports, water supplies and other public services like police and fire departments will need to be ready for this. Another thing to bear in mind is what your visitors are expecting as they make their way to your region or come and see your community. It's necessary to ensure that you are genuinely able to provide the tourists with what you have promised in any marketing schemes. Failure to do so can result in major losses in business as you may find it difficult to meet the visitors' expectations of quality products and services. Before attempting to market or advertise anything, it is important to know exactly what kind of tourist you are aiming to attract. This entails creating a visitor profile, starting by learning as much as you can about the people in and around your area. Once you know the demographics of your region and the surrounding areas, you can compare this to the type of people your event or venue will most likely attract.

Letting it be known

Essentially, cultural tourism works to satisfy the need to discover. It could be a new wine region or ancient artefacts, but cultural tourists travel because they feel the need to explore something that is completely unknown to them. Because they are travelling for the sheer experience and not merely because they happen to have vacation time, these tourists are usually willing to spend more money and travel more often. In addition to this as people work together to create a functional tourism industry a sense of community pride is established. This occurs as tourists get to see and explore various destinations in genuine and authentic ways.

Nowadays, people do research before they plan and book a trip or holiday. Therefore, it is important to have a functional method that people

NICHE TOURISM

can tap into to find out more about what you have to offer. Being online is a great way to make sure people have a point of reference. Ensuring that you are easy to find and that your chosen method of advertising is easy to navigate, will create a good initial impression of whatever it is you are offering to your potential visitors. An online presence can increase the chances of your event or location being seen by a large number of people. Other ways to advertise include flyers and posters at local hotels, cafes and restaurants.

Growing with the area

Local priorities generally differ with every region, which is why circumstances determine what each area can achieve with regards to cultural tourism. The programmes or venues that you may choose to offer a group of tourists need to therefore be realistic in relation to the resources available to you. How a region is marketed will depend on what kind of attractions are marketable, the talents of specific people and whether accommodation is readily available. In today's society, creative industries are being channelled to promote destinations and events while enhancing the competitiveness and attractiveness of the regions. As a local participating in the cultural tourism industry, you will need to ensure that you give tourists authentic representations of your histories and traditions.

A significant challenge facing cultural tourism is the task of preserving and protecting the actual culture that serves as a tourist attraction. It is important to protect the buildings, landscape or special places and qualities that can attract visitors. Another reason for this is the fact that local communities that would most likely be struggling economically can find financial support through maintaining and showing off their cultural assets. Locally, the participation of generally marginalised South Africans in the development of the tourist industry will afford them the chance to create businesses that can ensure the generation of income through tourist sales.

Taking on the challenge

One of the most notable setbacks faced by communities venturing into cultural tourism is the potential for exploitation of their area's cultural assets. Destroying these assets will in fact destroy the very things that attract the visitors in the first place. This is why collaboration plays a major role in cultural tourism. Regional partnerships allow for the development of themes, the pooling of resources and saving of money as the market potential expands. The active participation of political leaders, business leaders, operators of tourist sites, artists and craftspeople can result in very successful cultural tourism, as each sector of the community is given a chance to put its stamp on how their area is represented.

The part-time University of Cape Town Tourism Management short course is presented online throughout South Africa. Contact Nikki on 021 447 7565 or nicole@getsmarter.co.za for more information. Alternatively, visit www.GetSmarter.co.za

www.ingramcontent.com/pod-product-compliance
Lightning Source LLC
Chambersburg PA
CBHW041306180526
45172CB00003B/991